Steve Parish
NATURE Kids
KANGAROOS

MY FIRST
PICTURE
BOOK

www.steveparish.com.au

Kangaroos are mammals that have warm blood and breathe air. They grow hair and their babies feed on milk made by their mothers' body.

A kangaroo is a special kind of mammal called a marsupial.
Female marsupials have pouches for their tiny babies to grow in.

Most female kangaroos give birth to one baby at a time. The baby is called a joey. This big joey is drinking milk from inside its mother's pouch.

All kangaroos and their relatives belong to one family, the macropods. Macropod means "big footed". A kangaroo speeds along by bounding on its big feet.

All these animals are relatives of the kangaroo — a wallaroo, a bettong, a quokka, a potoroo and a tree-kangaroo.

Kangaroos and their relatives live all over Australia.
This is a rock-wallaby, which lives on rocky hillsides.

Large kangaroos eat grasses and the leaves of plants.
They sleep during the day, sometimes in the shade of a tree.

Kangaroos hop on their strong hind legs. They often have to travel long distances to find food and water.

This is a young tree-kangaroo. It uses its strong paws and rough-soled feet to climb. Tree-kangaroos eat the leaves of big, tropical rainforest trees.

Small kangaroos, such as potoroos and bettongs, dig up insects and plants from the ground. They need scrub or forests where the ground is soft and there are big plants to hide in or sleep under.

The Red Kangaroo and the Eastern Grey Kangaroo live in groups called mobs. This is a male Red Kangaroo. Most females are blue-grey.

During the day, Eastern Grey Kangaroos rest in the shade of trees and shrubs. From late afternoon to early morning they come out to feed. Their favourite food is grass.

Wallaroos live where there are steep hills. If they can get enough green grasses and plants to eat, they don't need to drink water.

Wallabies are small kangaroos. They may eat leaves as well as grass. Kangaroos and their relatives may be seen living free in the bush, or in zoos and wildlife parks.

A kangaroo

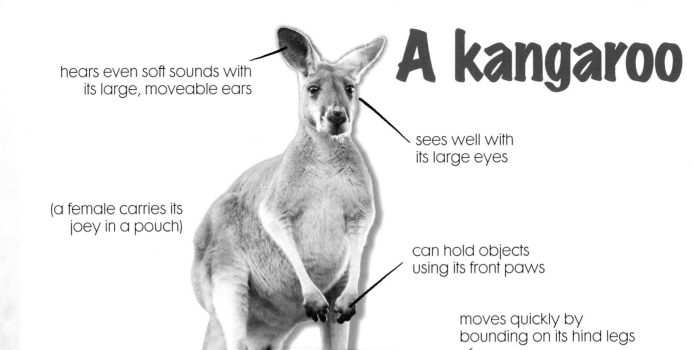

hears even soft sounds with its large, moveable ears

sees well with its large eyes

(a female carries its joey in a pouch)

can hold objects using its front paws

moves quickly by bounding on its hind legs

props itself up on its tail

Some zoos & fauna parks

QUEENSLAND
Cairns
Undersea World
Townsville
Great Barrier Reef Aquarium
Mooloolaba
Underwater World
Brisbane
Lone Pine Koala Sanctuary
Currumbin
Currumbin Sanctuary
Burleigh
Fleays Wildlife Park

NORTHERN TERRITORY
Berry Springs
Territory Wildlife Park
Alice Springs
Desert Wildlife Park

WESTERN AUSTRALIA
Perth
Perth Zoo
Hillarys
Underwater World
Karnup
Marapana Wildlife World

SOUTH AUSTRALIA
Adelaide
Adelaide Zoo
Mt Lofty
Cleland Wildlife Park
Mylor
Warrawong Sanctuary
Monarto
Monarto Zoo

VICTORIA
Melbourne
Melbourne Zoo
Healesville Sanctuary
Werribee Zoo
Phillip Island
Phillip Island Wildlife Park
Penguin Reserve
Seal Rocks

NEW SOUTH WALES
Dubbo
Western Plains Zoo
Sydney
Taronga Zoo
Sydney Aquarium

ACT
Canberra
Tidbinbilla Nature Reserve

TASMANIA
Brighton
Bonorong Park Wildlife Centre
Cygnet
Talune Wildlife Park & Koala Gardens
Mole Creek
Trowunna Wildlife Park